A souvenir guide

Osterley Park and House
Middlesex

Lucy Porten

National Trust

A Party Palace

Conveniently close to London, Osterley was fashioned for show and designed for entertaining.

'On Friday, we went to see – oh, the palace of palaces! – and yet a palace sans crown, sans coronet, but such expense! Such taste! Such profusion! … The old house I have often seen, which was built by Sir Thomas Gresham; but it is so improved and enriched, that all the Percies and Seymours of Sion must die of envy … There is a double portico that fills the space between the towers of the front, and is as noble as the Propyleum of Athens. There is a hall, library, breakfast room, eating room, all chefs d'oeuvre of Adam, a gallery 130 feet long, and a drawing room worthy of Eve before the Fall. Mrs. Child's dressing room is full of pictures, gold filigree, china and japan. So is all the house; the chairs are taken from antique lyres and make charming harmony; there are Salvators, Gaspar Poussins, and in the beautiful staircase, a ceiling by Rubens. Not to mention a kitchen-garden that costs £1,400 a year, a menagerie full of birds that come from a thousand islands.'

Horace Walpole to Lady Ossory, 21 June 1773

Above The east front of the mansion with its double portico

Key dates

1559	**Sir Thomas Gresham** acquires an estate in Heston, probably Osterley Farm
1564	**Queen Elizabeth I's** first visit to Osterley. Gresham completes the house the following year
1596	First known description of Osterley appears in **John Norden's** *Speculum Britanniae*
1635	First known image of Osterley appears in **Moses Glover's** *Survey of Isleworth*
1668	First known inventory of the contents of Osterley House made on the death of the then owner, **Sir William Waller**
1684	Osterley sold to **Nicholas Barbon** for £9,500
1713	**Sir Francis Child (the Elder)** acquires Osterley
1740	**Sir Francis Child (the Younger)** dies; his younger brother, **Samuel**, inherits
1756	Samuel's eldest son, **Francis**, comes of age and inherits Osterley and a vast fortune
1757	**Francis** acquires Upton House (now owned by the National Trust) for £17,000
1761	**Robert Adam** employed to modernise Osterley
1782	**Sarah Anne Child**, at 17 years old, elopes to marry John Fane, 10th Earl of Westmorland
1782	A full inventory of the contents of Osterley is made on the death of **Robert Child**
1804	**Sarah Sophia Child** marries George Villiers, 5th Earl of Jersey
1841	George Augustus Frederick Child, **6th Earl of Jersey** marries Julia, daughter of the Prime Minister Robert Peel
1859	Both the 6th and 7th Earls of Jersey die, leaving **Victor Albert George Villiers-Child** to inherit at the age of 14
1871	Osterley is let to the Dowager **Duchess of Cleveland**, daughter of the 9th Earl of Westmorland
1885	Eight-day sale of the Osterley **library** (including its nine Caxtons) raises £13,000
1923	**George Francis Child-Villiers** inherits Osterley at the age of 13
1939	George, the **9th Earl of Jersey**, opens Osterley to the public
1949	Osterley is gifted to the **National Trust** by the 9th Earl

Sir Thomas Gresham and Elizabethan Osterley

The grand red-brick Stable Block is the greatest survivor of Gresham's Osterley.

' The house nowe of the ladie Greshams, a faire and stately building of bricke, erected by Sir Thomas Gresham Knight, Citizen and Merchant Adventurer of London, and finished about anno 1577. It standeth in a parke by him also impaled, well wooded, and garnished with manie faire ponds, which afforded not onely fish and fowle, as swannes and other water fowle; but also great use of milles, as paper milles, oyle milles, and corne milles, all which are now decaied … In the same parke was a verie fair Heronie, for the increase and preservation whereof, sundrie allurements were devised and set up, fallen all to ruin.'

John Norden, *Speculum Britanniae*, 1596

Financial mastermind

Sir Thomas Gresham (?1519–79) served as a financial adviser to four Tudor monarchs. Described variously as financier, negotiator, merchant, diplomat, spy and philanthropist, he most famously founded the Royal Exchange in the City of London in 1565. With Queen Elizabeth and her Secretary of State, Lord Burghley, Gresham formed a powerful triumvirate, Thomas serving as a commercial agent, adviser and ambassador in Europe.

Above Sir Thomas Gresham; by Peter Scheemakers, c.1637, as depicted in the Temple of British Worthies in Stowe landscape garden

Left Gresham's stables (with later additions)

Thomas was the son of Sir Richard Gresham, a mercer who supplied tapestries to Cardinal Wolsey at Hampton Court, was knighted by Henry VIII and served both as Lord High Sheriff of the Tower of London and as Lord Mayor of London. Thomas was sent to Cambridge and then into apprenticeship with his uncle, Sir John, as a merchant adventurer.

Gresham acquired a licence to enclose 600 acres at Osterley in 1565. At that time it is likely that there was little more than a farmhouse here. He quickly acquired more land, improved the estate, developed it to generate income (establishing one of the first paper mills in England) and embellished the house.

Gresham's Osterley

It is difficult to say with certainty what Gresham's Osterley looked like. Described as 'beseeming a prince', the only surviving view appears in Moses Glover's 1635 survey of Isleworth. This shows a nearly square, two-storeyed house with an attic in a steep, hipped roof and a turreted skyline with waving banners. The principal front faced east to a fountain courtyard. In the internal angles of the courtyard stood four tall turrets, almost certainly containing staircases. Beyond is depicted a fenced park, which extended from the River Brent to the east and to Heston to the

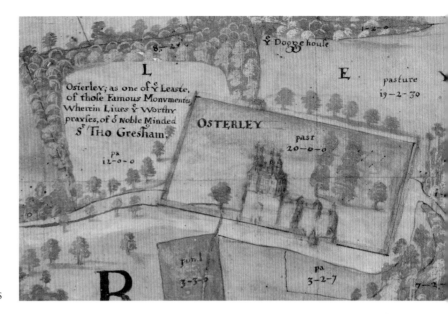

west, containing six rectangular ponds and a tall hunting lodge with another turreted roof.

Thwarted ambitions

Alas, Gresham's plans to establish a dynasty were cruelly thwarted when his only son, Richard, died of the fever in 1564 at the age of 20. Instead, following the death of his wife, Anne, Gresham House in Bishopsgate, London, became Gresham College, generously endowed by his will.

Above Detail from Moses Glover's 1635 Survey of Isleworth, which provides the only surviving contemporary view of Gresham's house (collection of Syon House)

A royal visitor
Elizabeth I visited Osterley many times, staying overnight in the house for the first time in 1564. For that visit, Gresham commissioned Sir Thomas Churchyard to write a pageant. Thomas Fuller, in his *History of the Worthies of England*, relates, 'Her Majesty found fault with the Court of this House as too great, affirming, That it would appear more handsome, if divided with a Wall in the middle', Sir Thomas, during the night, sent for workmen, who 'so speedily apply their business, That the next morning discovered that Court double, which the night had left single before.'

The Child family and 18th-century Osterley

Above Sir William Waller, a Parliamentary general who owned Osterley at the time of his death in 1668; by Cornelius Johnson (National Portrait Gallery)

Right *Temple Bar;* by John Collett, *c*.1760. The business premises of Child & Co were nearby at 1 Fleet Street (Jersey Loan)

Opposite Sir Francis Child the Elder (1642-1713) in his robes as Lord Mayor; circle of Sir Godfrey Kneller (Christ's Hospital, Horsham). Both Sir Francis Child the Elder and his son, Francis the Younger, served as Presidents of Christ's Hospital

For the next century, following Sir Thomas Gresham's death in 1579, Osterley passed through numerous hands.

An inventory of Sir William Waller's goods and chattels, made at his death in 1668, lists 46 rooms at Osterley, including a painted gallery, great parlour and bedchambers hung with tapestries and velvet. After further brief ownerships, Osterley was bought, early in 1684, by Nicholas Barbon for £9,500.

Nicholas Barbon (1637/40–98)

Doctor, economist, financier, building speculator and entrepreneur, Barbon was also the founder of fire insurance in England – capitalising on the Great Fire of London of 1666. To own Gresham's estate must have delighted such an ambitious opportunist: he had even tried to establish a land bank to rival the Bank of England and to sell pumped drinking water from the River Thames. Barbon raised a huge mortgage against Osterley and began making sizeable alterations. He died, in debt, in 1698. Francis Child, one of Barbon's creditors, acquired the estate some 15 years later.

A family of goldsmiths and bankers

Francis Child the Elder (1642-1713) was born in Wiltshire, the son of a prosperous clothier. Following an apprenticeship as a goldsmith, he joined the firm of Robert Blanchard. Blanchard had recently married Margaret Wheeler, widow and heir of an extremely successful goldsmith and, in 1671, Francis Child married her daughter, Elizabeth, who, in time, would inherit the combined Wheeler and Blanchard fortunes.

Like many goldsmiths, the firm had developed from respected craftsmen into money lenders and custodians of deposited valuables. By the 1660s, roughly a third of all Blanchard's new accounts were devoted to banking rather than goldsmithing transactions, and his shop at Temple Bar was extended by acquiring adjoining premises at 1 Fleet Street.

The site was marked by a street sign (common in the largely illiterate 16th and 17th centuries) of a Marygold. This flower would become the sign under which Child & Co. would operate. Banking, goldsmithing and a certain amount of property speculation made Francis Child a rich man. As his wealth increased, so too did his participation and standing in City affairs. He was appointed 'jeweller in ordinary' to William III, represented Devizes in parliament, became Lord Mayor of London and was knighted. Sir Francis purchased a substantial town house in Lincoln's Inn Fields (where he hung his art collection, which included paintings by Rubens, Claude, Guido Reni and Van Dyck) and, not long before his death, acquired Osterley.

Sir Francis, who had twelve children, was succeeded by his three surviving sons: Robert, Francis and Samuel, each of whom would inherit Osterley and live there. Both Robert (1674–1721) and Francis (known as the Younger; 1684–1740) were MPs, knighted, and served as directors of the family bank and of the East India Company. Both also made alterations to Osterley, conservatively transforming the Tudor house into something befitting its rich owners and the tastes of their time.

Above 'At the sign of the Marygold'. Sir Francis Child traded under this hanging sign in Fleet Street

Left Francis Child III
(1735–63); by Allan Ramsay
(Jersey Loan)

A new generation

Samuel died in 1752, but his eldest surviving son, the third Francis Child (1735–63), did not come of age until 1756. After more than half a century a new generation was in charge, one very different from the last – more educated, more cultivated, less inclined to work in the family business, but still incredibly rich. Within seven years of inheriting, Francis had bought a new country house at Upton in Warwickshire (now also owned by the National Trust), acquired a large and valuable library, become engaged and had employed the fashionable architect Robert Adam to create a house more befitting his status and entertainments.

Alas, in September 1763, on the eve of his wedding to Maria Constantina Trevor, Francis died suddenly. His brother, Robert (1739–82), inherited Osterley and, no doubt with sadness, continued with his own marriage plans, taking Sarah Jodrell of Ankerwycke House as his bride only a fortnight later. While Osterley remained the family's principal residence, Robert sold their house in Lincoln's Inn Fields, acquiring a larger and more fashionable one at 38 Berkeley Square from the Duke of Manchester. The family lived at Osterley from June to November, spent the winter season in London and used their country house, Upton, for hunting and shooting.

The runaway bride

Robert died, at the age of 43, in July 1782, just two months after his only child, Sarah Anne (1764–93), aged 17, slipped out of their London home and eloped with the racy John Fane, 10th Earl of Westmorland, a neighbour in Berkeley Square. Robert forgave his daughter, giving his consent to a second, private marriage at Lord Westmorland's seat in Northamptonshire, Apethorpe. The terms of his will, however, prohibited the sale or significant alteration of Osterley and left the whole of his fortune, not to his daughter, nor her first born, but to her second child, male or female, thereby ensuring it did not pass to the main branch of the Westmorland family.

In time, Robert's widow, Sarah, remarried (becoming Lady Ducie in 1791) and her daughter, Lady Westmorland, gave birth to first a son, John, and then, in 1785, a daughter, Sarah Sophia – the heir to all the Child properties and fortune (see family tree on outside front cover fold out).

Above left Robert Child (1739–82); by George Romney (Jersey Loan)

Above right Sarah Jodrell (c.1740–93), who married Robert Child in 1763; by George Romney (Jersey Loan)

Left Robert and Sarah Child with their daughter, Sarah Anne (1764–3); by Margaret Battine after Daniel Gardner

The Child-Villiers family and 19th-century Osterley

During the 19th century Osterley was home to three formidable women.

'Queen Sarah'

Sarah Sophia (1785–1867) was only eight when she inherited Osterley and the Child fortune in 1793, both her mother and grandmother having died in the same year. By the time she came of age in 1806, she was the Countess of Jersey, having married George Villiers (pronounced 'Villers'), 5th Earl of Jersey in 1804. His family

home, Middleton Park in Oxfordshire, became their principal residence, and country life suited them. The Earl, who served as Master of the Horse to Queen Victoria, was a dedicated supporter of horse racing, owning, breeding and training his own horses at Middleton, including three Derby winners.

The Countess of Jersey, meanwhile, was a great society hostess, a regular on the London scene and a leader of fashion. Using the 60-room family town house in Berkeley Square as a base, Sarah Sophia astounded London with her extravagant lifestyle. 'Queen Sarah', as she was commonly known, was one of the six lady patronesses of Almack's, a London club almost as exclusive as the Court. She was painted by Lawrence and Romney, was immortalised as Zenobia in Disraeli's novel *Endymion* and ridiculed in Caroline Lamb's *Glenarvon*.

Osterley at risk

The family grew. The couple's eldest son, George August Frederick (1808–59), married Julia, daughter of the Prime Minister, Sir Robert Peel. Even for the wealthy Jerseys, though, Osterley was expensive to maintain, and activities on the turf did not come cheap. In 1818, 1829 and again in 1832 the family attempted to let Osterley with no success, and the despairing Earl explored the possibility of building villas in the park. Sadly, the couple's eldest son (of seven children), George, died barely three weeks after his father in 1859. The 5th Earl's grandson, Victor Albert George (1845–1915), therefore inherited the title as the 7th Earl of Jersey at the age of 14.

Left 'Queen Sarah'. Sarah Sophia, Countess of Jersey; after James Holmes (National Portrait Gallery)

Repairing Osterley

Despite her care, the 1884 Schedule of Dilapidation describes an Osterley evidently in need of considerable repair and renovation. Although the 7th Earl of Jersey (1845–1915) was appointed Governor of New South Wales the following year, his wife Margaret (1849–1945) embarked on an extensive programme of repair and refurbishment. An eight-day sale of the great Fairfax Library raised over £13,000 for the most urgent works. The Entrance Hall and Library were redecorated; the State Bedroom hung with pleated silk; the Etruscan Dressing Room used as a school-room for her children. The garden party held in the summer of 1884 proved a great success and weekend parties soon became regular. Princes, politicians, writers and leading public figures all came as Osterley returned to its role as pleasure palace.

Left Grace Caroline Lowther, Dowager Duchess of Cleveland in old age; lithograph published in *Vanity Fair,* 1883 (National Portrait Gallery)

Below left Margaret, Countess of Jersey, dressed as Anne of Austria for the Devonshire House Ball, 1897 (National Portrait Gallery)

A tenant for Osterley

Finally, in 1871, a tenant for Osterley was found, and £3,200 spent on refurbishing the house. Grace Caroline Lowther, Dowager Duchess of Cleveland, was the widow of William Vane, 3rd Duke of Cleveland and the niece of John Fane, 10th Earl of Westmorland. Augustus Hare, the writer and raconteur, wrote of her after a visit in 1879:

'I came to Osterley yesterday, most kindly welcomed by the good old Duchess of Cleveland, who is delightful. The greatness of her charm certainly lies in the absence of charm: no one ever had less of it. But what bright intelligence, what acute perceptions, what genuine kindness, what active beneficence!'

For the next 13 years, until her death in 1883, Grace loved and cared for the house, incessantly offering hospitality and 'stumping about with her ebony stick'.

The 9th Earl of Jersey

George Francis Child-Villiers (1910–98) was 13 years old when he became the 9th Earl of Jersey.

In 1934, at just 24, he began remodelling Middleton, the family home in Oxfordshire, commissioning Sir Edwin Lutyens and his son, Robert. During the works, he and his wife moved into Osterley. By 1937 his first marriage, to Patricia Richards, an Australian debutante, had ended. His second wife was Virginia Cherrill, an actress who had famously played the blind flower girl in Charlie Chaplin's *City Lights* (1931) and had been married to Cary Grant previously.

A wonderful place for a party
Osterley, again, proved itself a wonderful place for entertaining and in 1939 a magnificent Georgian Ball was held. With an Executive Committee including the designers Oliver Messel and Felix Harbord and under the patronage of Queen Mary, the Ball attracted the most glamorous crowd.

'In the white and scarlet tent, designed by Oliver Messel, the company danced – countesses and peers, film-stars and socialites, architects and Mr Osbert Lancaster. The band peeped from a frame of bamboo and wreathed ivy, lights were concealed in sheaves of corn, corner pedestals were crowned with plaster horses' heads, their purple manes tied with green ribbons.'

Left The poster for the 1939
Georgian Ball was designed
by Oliver Messel

A collector of Impressionist paintings himself, he organised an exhibition of contemporary art on the upper floor. Paintings by Augustus John, Duncan Grant, Vanessa Bell and L.S. Lowry were shown alongside sculptural works by Frank Dobson and Sir William Reid Dick in the Chinese and Indian Rooms. Between 26 May and 2 September 1939, 19,000 people visited the house, and 27,000 the grounds.

It was clear, however, that Lord Jersey would not reside permanently at Osterley again – a fact brought into sharp focus when he and his family sold Middleton and moved to Jersey in 1948. He remained insistent that the house and contents should be preserved intact. Finally, in 1949, the 9th Earl gave the estate to the National Trust.

Opposite George,
9th Earl of Jersey
photographed by Bassano
in 1931 (National Portrait
Gallery)

Left The poster for the 1939
Georgian Ball was designed
by Oliver Messel

Below Lord and Lady Jersey
at the Georgian Ball, 1939

The fête champêtre included an 18th-century beer-garden, a hermit in the Grotto, wrestling and a fireworks display above the lake, while below musicians dressed as gondoliers played Handel's *Water Music* from a raft. Lord Jersey wore a blue velvet suit copied from the one worn by Francis Child in the portrait by Ramsay (see p.18), while Lady Jersey came as the 4th Countess, in a dress of blue and silver designed by Messel. The Countess of Rosse (Oliver Messel's sister and mother of the Earl of Snowdon), was reported to have sported blue hair, blue eyelashes and blue eyelids!

Opening Osterley
In the same year, Lord Jersey (known as 'Grandy' from his previous courtesy title, Viscount Grandison) also opened Osterley to the public.

Robert Adam

The Adam style

Although, as was often the case, Robert Adam (1728–92) was called upon to alter an existing house, a great deal of the significance of Osterley lies in his contribution. He is responsible both for its external appearance, with the dramatic transparent double portico, and its incomparable Neo-classical interiors. Moreover, Adam was engaged here from at least 1761 until 1780, allowing, in one house, a rare display of his evolving style – from its early robustness to its later, more fluent delicacy. By the 1780s many of his more obvious decorative features had been taken over by contemporary designers, though seldom with his understanding of their syntax. By his death, the *Gentleman's Magazine* could claim that he had 'produced a total change in the architecture of this country'. Today, 'Adam' as an adjective may still be found in the dictionary, so much has his decorative style become part of British architectural history and language.

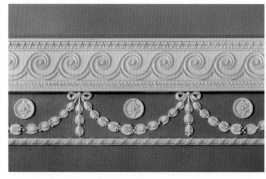

'Of all Robert Adam's great palaces where he worked over a number of years in embellishing state apartments, Osterley affords the best example of his comparative styles side by side under one roof. Above all it is distinguished for fidelity of execution in accordance with the architect's drawings and for its wealth of original furnishings. In this last respect it transcends even Harewood, Kedleston and Syon.'

James Lees-Milne, *The Age of Adam*, 1947

The Grand Tour

Robert was the second son of William Adam (1689–1748), Scotland's most distinguished and successful architect. William and his wife, Mary, had ten children, including sons, John (the eldest, who inherited the practice), Robert and James, who went into business together. At 26 Robert travelled to Rome. During the next four years he made his Grand Tour, enjoying continental life, studying its buildings, making aristocratic connections and meeting other artists and architects, including Giovanni Battista Piranesi and Charles-Louis Clérisseau, who acted as Adam's guide to the antiquities and teacher in draughtsmanship. Like others undertaking this cultural pilgrimage, he carefully studied the antique, diligently measuring and sketching both ancient and Renaissance buildings. In short, it was during these years that the foundations of his career and his style were built.

The height of fashion

Upon his return, in 1758, Adam settled in London, buying a house in Mayfair, joining the recently established Royal Society of Arts and building a practice. His self-confidence, private means and command of classical antiquity all aided his cause, and his work quickly became fashionable. A flurry of high-status commissions followed: Hatchlands (now also owned by the National Trust), Surrey, for Admiral Boscawen; Harewood House, near Leeds, for the 1st Baron Harewood; Croome Court (NT), Worcestershire, for the 6th Earl of Coventry; Kedleston (NT), Derbyshire for Sir Nathaniel Curzon; Syon, west London, for the Earl (later Duke) of Northumberland.

It is unknown how, and by whom, Adam was first introduced to the Child family and Osterley, but by 1761 he was in their employ. His task – to modernise the house – was not an easy one.

Opposite above **Robert Adam in the early 1770s; attributed to George Willison (National Portrait Gallery)**

Opposite below **Vitruvian (wave) scrolls and swags ornament the Stairs**

Left **The door furniture was designed by Adam, as used at Kedleston Hall and Saltram**

Below **Adam's laid-out wall elevations for the Eating Room**

Exploring Osterley

The evolution of the house before
Robert Adam's involvement is perplexing.

Above The house from
across the lake

Above The house from
across the lake

Below Sunflowers feature
on the ceiling of the portico

It is possible that for all its subsequent owners, Osterley's association with Sir Thomas Gresham still resonated and influenced their retention of so much of his original house and stables. Certainly, materials were reused, and older features retained.

It is reasonable to assume that no comprehensive plan existed before Adam's engagement in the 1760s. Nicholas Barbon's ambitious plans for Osterley rendered the house practically uninhabitable for much of the 1690s. Its acquisition by the Child family most probably brought conservative, piecemeal improvements.

From Adam's survey drawing of the south front of the house (c.1760), we know that the windows were irregularly spaced with Venetian frames at both ends of the Long Gallery and that there was a grand Tuscan doorway (probably serving as the entrance at some stage). While accounts show that one family of carpenters, the Hillyards, served the family across all their properties during this period, another architect may also have been involved. Certainly, the sculptor Joseph Wilton carved the marble chimneypieces in the Gallery to a design by the architect William Chambers, but there is no more conclusive evidence of the latter's involvement.

John Rocque's map suggests that by the 1740s the front entrance was aligned to the centre of the east side of the house. It seems likely that Sir Francis the Younger raised the height of the house, replacing the attic with a proper third

The collection

In August 1782, following the death of Robert Child, an inventory of the contents of Osterley Park was made.

By this date, Adam had completed his work in the house, so the contents as created by him are fully listed. More fortunate still is the survival of so many of those contents in their original positions.

Together again

Had the 9th Earl of Jersey executed his original intention to gift the entire estate, house and contents to the National Trust, it would have been second only to Petworth in its magnificence as a gift. Alas, in the end, the indigenous pictures were not presented in 1949, and for many years Osterley was dependent on loans to complete the Adam interiors with paintings. Fortunately, in 2013, 65 years after their removal, 24 indigenous pictures (together with a similar number of pieces of furniture) returned to Osterley on loan from the Jersey Trust and George Child-Villiers, 10th Earl of Jersey (b.1976).

storey, creating a *piano nobile* (principal floor) and making this entrance, while his brother, Samuel, added the two turrets on this façade (to mirror those on the west) soon after.

It is, however, Adam's dramatic and unusual transparent portico, forming a classical entrance between the romantic red of the Tudor brick, that creates the most iconic image of Osterley. Designed in 1763, Walpole considered this entrance 'as noble as the Propyleum at Athens', the gateway to the Acropolis in Athens. Above, on the triangular tympanum, a laurel-wreathed medallion depicts a Roman marriage flanked by tripod torchères supported by griffins – majestic, mythical beasts set to guard the house and its treasures.

Right Heraldic Child eagles flank the front steps

The Entrance Hall

Adam was faced with a space ill proportioned for his need and desire to create a room of suitable spectacle and status.

So his design (with semi-domed niches at each end, repetitive, elongated pilasters and a truncated entablature) aims to shorten the length of the room, emphasises the vertical, and gives the illusion of a higher ceiling. Adam, here, also introduces emblems and motifs that will reappear throughout his rooms on the principal floor.

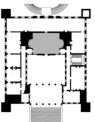

Gods and goddesses

In the four great alcoves stand, to the left, Apollo, god of poetry and music, and Minerva, goddess of the arts; to the right, Ceres, goddess of plenty and the harvest, and Hercules, hero and god of labourers, the apples of Hesperides in one hand and his gnarled club in the other. Between them two grisaille (monochromatic) painted panels by Giovanni Battista Cipriani (1727–85) depict *The Triumph of Bacchus* and *The Triumph of Ceres*. Bacchus taught mankind to cultivate the vine, Ceres the earth. Osterley is thus immediately portrayed as not only a temple to the arts, but also a celebration of abundance through labour.

Arms and armour

On the far wall, four stucco panels display trophies of armour. These recall the long tradition of displaying arms in country houses (from a time when every house of size had reserves of armour, but, by this time, with no practical function). They also refer to the antique marble trophies of the Emperor Augustus on the Campidoglio in Rome. The frieze and pilasters reference Emperor Diocletian's Palace at Spalato, which Adam had studied a decade before in 1757.

Furnishings and flooring

Both the four hall stools with scroll ends and the pair of carved wood brackets with vase-shaped girandoles (on the window wall) can also be attributed to Robert Adam. Presumably, so too the floor of white Portland and red sandstone, which answers his ceiling design in reverse, though no drawing survives.

Decoration

Accounts show that the painter David Adamson decorated the Hall in 'three tints grey' in 1787. By the early 20th century the decoration had been picked out in blue and white and renamed the 'Wedgwood Hall'. The French grey with white scheme of today reflects its original form, described, in 1772, as having white ornaments on a 'ground of greenish light grey'.

Little is missing from the room as recorded by the inventory of 1782 bar 'a marble reclining Magdalen' and 'a marble sleeping Jesus' (as well as two large India Umbrellas and a telescope on a mahogany stand).

Above One of the stucco panels of military trophies

Left The Portland stone chimneypieces depict the Child family crest of an eagle holding an adder in its beak

Opposite The Entrance Hall

The Eating Room

In his *Works in Architecture,* of 1772, Adam described English eating rooms as:

'apartments of conversation, in which we are to pass a great deal of our time. This renders it desirable to have them fitted up with elegance and splendour, but in a style different from that of other apartments. Instead of being hung with damask, tapestry &c. they are always finished with stucco, and adorned with statues and paintings, that they may not retain the smell of the victuals.'

Here, as is traditional, emblems appropriate for an eating room abound.

Appropriate for eating

The ceiling is decorated with grape-clustered vines, wine ewers and thyrsi (ivy-wreathed staffs tipped with an ornament resembling a pine cone, carried by the followers of Bacchus, the god of wine).

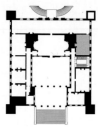

Left Over the chimneypiece is Cipriani's *An Offering to Ceres*

Bottom left Acanthus scroll wall decoration in the Eating Room

Symbol of plenty

Above the chimneypiece *An Offering to Ceres*, goddess of plenty, is depicted by Giovanni Battista Cipriani (1727–85), while elsewhere the stucco frames flanked by arabesque panes contain paintings by Antonio Zucchi (1726–95). They feature festive scenes of celebration including a Roman marriage, a wedding feast and Turkish figures dancing among classical ruins. The four overdoors represent the four known Continents.

Displaying gold and silver

The complex, carved and gilt mahogany sideboard was designed by Adam and made by John Linnell as part of a theatrical display of gold and silver, including a huge silver wine cooler which stood underneath (now displayed in the Strong Room) – a reminder that the Child family were wealthy goldsmith bankers. The table is flanked by a pair of ormolu-mounted mahogany vases on round, white and gilt fluted pedestals; one would have held a mahogany pail, the other a chamberpot. En suite on the window wall are two pier tables with 'antique' marble mosaic tops with accompanying oval pier-glasses, designed by Adam in 1767, their gilt frames decorated with husk festoons.

Above The Eating Room

Making charming harmony

Twelve mahogany chairs with lyre backs, designed by Adam and almost certainly made by Linnell, were admired by Walpole when he visited in 1773. They were designed to stand against the walls when not in use – three each side of the chimneypiece, one each side of the sideboard, two armchairs in the end windows with the last four against the remaining wall. Similarly, the inventory of 1782 confirms that three dining tables, one with a leather cover, were kept in the adjoining North Passage, for use in this room when required.

The carpet, rewoven by the V&A, is a copy of the 19th-century one, itself a copy of the 18th-century original.

The Library

'The Library is a charming room, It is fill'd with fine Books, and Mr Adams
[sic] has lavished all his taste in ornamenting every part. it is plain white
with Tables, Desks, & chairs are all of the fine inlaid work of different
woods, and you cannot imagine how very elegant they are, and must
have cost a great deal of money, but indeed one sees that no expence has
been spared anywhere.'

Agneta Yorke in a letter to Lady Beauchamp Proctor, 1772

The Fairfax collection

Almost immediately upon inheriting his fortune in 1756, Francis Child (the third) acquired the large and valuable library of Brian Fairfax. Fairfax, a friend of Lord Burlington's, was a cousin by marriage of both Francis and George Villiers, Duke of Buckingham. The magnificent library, a collection of over 2,000 books, included nine printed by William Caxton. It was eventually sold, over eight days, by the family in 1885, raising over £13,000 and enabling them to save the house.

The ceiling and frieze

Adam produced at least three alternative designs for the ceiling, including two coloured, while the stony white of the bookcases, with their Ionic Order frontispieces, are thoroughly architectural. The uniting frieze patterned with circles, bell-flowers and rosettes is repeated round the walls, over the doors and on the chimneypieces.

Appropriate decoration

The coloured paintings inserted into the decorative scheme are by the Venetian Antonio Zucchi (1726–95), who had travelled with Adam in Italy. Until his marriage to Angelica Kauffman

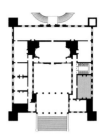

Opposite **The Library**

Below left **One of the Library chimneypieces**

Left **The marquetry on the Library desk represents painting**

in 1781 and their move to Rome, he remained Adam's principal decorative painter. The pictures, very appropriately, allude to the Arts and Sciences and include: *Britannia Encouraging and Rewarding Arts and Sciences* (over the door); *Anacreon Sacrificing to the Graces* (over mantel to the left); *Pythagoras Restoring Birds and Fishes to their Former Freedom; The Muse of Ovid Delivering a Feather Taken from the Wing of Love* and *Apollo and Minerva on Mount Parnassus in the Company of the Muses.* The plaster medallions depict the Greek poets Homer and Hesiod and the Roman authors Horace and Cicero.

Furnishings

The ormolu-mounted marquetry furniture of the very highest quality is thought to have been supplied by the Linnell workshop. The remarkably sophisticated French Neo-classical style can be credited to the Swedish cabinet-maker Georg Haupt, who designed a very similar medal cabinet. The large desk bears marquetry trophies to architecture, sculpture, art and music (a lyre echoing those forming the splats of the *en suite* armchairs). The Vitruvian wave scroll frieze unites the desks and chairs.

The Yellow Breakfast Room

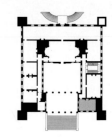

'The Breakfast room is Lemon colour, with blew ornaments, the Chairs Mrs Childs own work, in very elegant frames, in quite a new taste, the walls are hung full of pictures, and the beautiful portrait of Mrs Child, by Cotes is over the Chimney.'

Agneta Yorke in a letter to Lady Beauchamp Proctor, 1772

It is not hard to imagine mornings spent here, its windows affording some of the best views of the park and lakes.

It was described in 1782 as the Breakfast Room with both a pembroke table and an inlaid tea chest. A daytime sitting room used as a waiting room for visitors, it was also decorated with a dense picture hang of 41 works in gilt frames, including paintings by Claude Lorraine, Nicolas Poussin, Canaletto and Sir Joshua Reynolds.

Left Sarah Anne Child was a favourite pupil of the Italian composer Gabriel Piozzi; by George Dance (National Portrait Gallery)

Opposite Sarah Anne Child's harpsichord

Much of the decorative work pre-dates Adam, whose only contribution is the pair of pier-tables and pier-glasses, dated 1777.

Sarah Anne's harpsichord

The room also housed then, as today, a harpsichord in a mahogany case. It was supplied in 1781 by the celebrated maker, Jacob Kirckman, and his nephew Abraham (whose signatures are inscribed on a tablet set into the nameboard) and is decorated with lavish marquetry depicting flowers and seaweed, musical instruments and manuscript pages as well as two winged figures with trumpets to their lips. It was probably made for Sarah Anne Child (1764–93), a favourite pupil of Gabriel Piozzi, the Italian singer and composer, who dedicated a set of six sonatas to her. After her early death in 1793, the instrument was sent to her grieving husband, the Earl of Westmorland. Returned to Osterley in 1805, when their daughter was refurnishing the house, it was removed once more by the family, when the property was gifted to the National Trust in 1949. In 1993 it formed part of the Jersey bequest, making its return permanent.

The Long Gallery

The Long Gallery occupies the
entire length of the garden front
of the house.

The birth of the Gallery

Galleries are first recorded in large houses
and castles during the Tudor era.
Originating from covered walks, early
examples often came in pairs, one above
the other, the higher closed in and the
lower open, both looking into the garden.
Probably intended as protected ways
leading from one place to another, they
soon became places of indoor exercise.
Over time they gradually increased in
pretension, as hangings and paintings
began to find their place on the walls.
By 1547 Henry VIII had 19 pictures hanging
in his Long Gallery at Hampton Court; by
1668 Sir William Waller had 24 hanging in
his painted Long Gallery at Osterley.

When the Childs' London house was sold in 1767,
the impressive collection of pictures acquired
by Sir Francis a century before was moved to
Osterley. The 1782 inventory lists 49 paintings
in the Gallery. They included two gigantic
equestrian portraits – one of the 1st Duke of
Buckingham by Rubens, the other of Charles I
after Van Dyck – hung, in imitation of the King's
Gallery at Kensington Palace, facing each other
from the far ends of the room. Besides these,
the room contained works by Titian, Poussin,
Sir Peter Lely, Claude Lorraine and Salvator
Rosa. Sadly, Lord Jersey's gift of Osterley in
1949 did not include the paintings. Sadder still,
a great many were lost in a fire *en route* to his
home in Jersey the same year. The present
hang is, therefore, largely dependent on loans;
designed by Alastair Laing, then the National
Trust's Curator of Paintings and Sculpture, it
reflects the 18th-century hang.

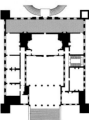

Above The Long Gallery

A profusion of sofas

By the 19th century the Gallery looked very different. Sarah Spencer, Lady Lyttelton, writing to her brother in 1809, described its size 'and yet by means of two large chimney pieces, and a profusion of sofas, chairs and tables of all sizes, a billiard table, books, pictures, and a pianoforte, it was as comfortable and as well filled as a small room would.' By the time of Lady Jersey's Saturday-to-Monday parties at Osterley, the American writer Henry James, a frequent visitor, described the room as 'a cheerful upholstered avenue into another century', under the name Summersoft in his novella of 1888, *The Lesson of the Master.* Lit by 400 candles reflected in the mirrors that run the entire length of the room, it is not hard to imagine how dazzling evening receptions must have been.

The large, central Ionic doorcase into the Entrance Hall is copied from an engraving in Isaac Ware's *Designs of Inigo Jones* (1731), and probably dates from the 1730s or 1740s. The frieze, which incorporates the sign of the Childs Bank, the marigold, may date from the same time. The marble chimneypieces were carved by the sculptor Joseph Wilton, who procured the designs from the architect William Chambers.

Adam's furnishings

Adam designed the four pier-glasses and six large girandoles with unusual heart-shaped glasses, all of which were almost certainly made by John Linnell. The latter can also be credited with the earlier suite of 12 mahogany armchairs and six large settees (their seat rails matching the dado; their legs echoing the chimneypieces). Originally, the suite was covered with 'pea Green silk and Stuff Damask' to match the colour of the walls. The two long sofas that now reside on the end walls were reupholstered in the 1880s. The embroidery depicts, on one, the sign of the Child Bank (the sun shining on a marigold); on the other, the Jersey arms.

Left Adam was able to reproduce the carved and gilt-wood girandoles following the success of those he had designed for the Child family's London house in Berkeley Square

Right An 18th-century Chinese pagoda mounted with mother of pearl and decorated with silver bells

An imperial barge
The mid-18th-century Chinese imperial junks (the dragon representing the emperor; the phoenix the empress), and the pagodas were here in 1782. The large parade (or mandarin) jars were described as 'tremendous Japanese vases … large enough to conceal Carl' (her younger brother) by the German tourist Sophie von la Roche, when she visited in 1786.

The Drawing Room

'… out of this Gallery we are conducted into the drawing room which is a beautiful room, hung with pea-green damask, furniture the same, the ceiling is extremely elegant, painted & gilt, and the carpet, which is from Mr Moores manufactory answers to the ceiling; there are some fine pictures in this room also …'

Agneta Yorke in a letter to Lady Beauchamp Proctor, 1772

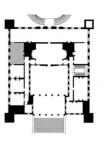

Paintings

In the 1782 inventory the Drawing Room was described as 'hung round with peagreen silk Damask and gilt metal border'. It contained 'an oval portrait of Vandyke by Himself' paired with 'An oval Portrait of Dobson by Himself'. The former was acquired, after a national fundraising campaign, by the National Portrait Gallery in 2015. The latter is currently on loan to the National Trust from the Jersey family, having returned here in 2013. Both were acquired in 1712 by Sir Francis Child from the collector Richard Graham and date from the 1640s. The *Self-portrait* of William Dobson, painted in his distinctive style, clearly imitates the earlier piece by Van Dyck and both have exceptional and elaborate auricular (ear-shaped) frames.

Here too hang various portraits of the Child family, including Robert Child and his wife, Sarah, painted by George Romney in 1781–2. *The Music Lesson* by Sir Peter Lely, recorded in the Gallery in 1782, was at the Childs' Oxfordshire home, Middleton, by 1867.

Opulent Adam

It is fitting that such paintings were displayed in such an opulent room. Here Adam's hand can be seen everywhere, and drawings for wall elevations, ceiling, carpet, commode details, pier-glass, chimneypiece and even the grate and fender survive in the collections of Osterley and the Sir John Soane's Museum. The ceiling design is inspired by an illustration of the coffering of the Temple of the Sun at Palmyra. While it is one of the most celebrated instances of Adam borrowing from antiquity, it is the only instance of his using the Temple as a model and its meaning for the Child family may have lain more in the *trompe-l'oeil* version found in the nave of West Wycombe church, painted for Sir Francis Dashwood, later Lord Le Despenser. It is quite possible that Dashwood introduced Adam to the banker family. The carpet, its floral motifs in circular garlands reflecting the ceiling above, was designed by Adam around 1768. It was made by Thomas Moore of Moorfields.

Ornamental commodes

The pair of hollow commodes designed by Adam serves no practical purpose. Veneered with hardwood, satinwood and rosewood and with ormolu mounts, their exquisite decoration incorporates marquetry medallions thought to have been made by the Swedish craftsman Christopher Fürloh. Taken from engravings after paintings by Angelica Kauffman, one portrays *Diana with her hounds,* the other *Venus explaining to Cupid the torch of Hymen.* They are flanked by marquetry panels representing antique candlesticks. Here too are the ever-present griffins (flanking medallions on the commodes and repeated on the fireplace transom, pier-glasses and doorframes), while the frieze echoes those on the doorcases, and the arcaded base the frieze round the room.

Decoration

Walpole admired the 'admirable effect' created by the dark crimson of the ceiling against the pale green of the original wall coverings. The original damask was replaced in the 19th century. The set of eight gilt armchairs and two sofas was supplied by Linnell around 1769. It was originally upholstered in the same pea green silk damask as the walls and was re-covered in the 1970s.

Mantelpiece vases

The 1782 inventory also lists seven spar vases, presumably, as today, decorating the mantelpiece. The two spar vases with double branches may be identified with the pair of blue john vases with winged female caryatids bought by Robert Child in 1772 from Matthew Boulton.

The Tapestry Room

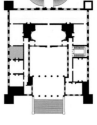

Commissioned and installed under the direction of Robert Adam, 18 separate pieces of tapestry cover the walls in this room, together with complementary tapestry chair covers, fire-screen and chimney board.

Ordered around 1772, they were delivered to Osterley some four years later by the Gobelins factory in Paris, which had been established as a royal tapestry manufactory under Louis XIV (1638–1715). By this time, the firm was under the entrepreneur Jacques Neilson, a Scot by origin, and it is his name that can be seen signed on the tapestry above the chimneypiece.

François Boucher (1703–70), the French painter, had been appointed designer-in-chief at Gobelins in 1755. The designs for the painted roundels in the wall tapestries are his, and the series became known as the *Tenture de Boucher* ('Tenture' being the French word for a series of tapestry designs).

The tapestry design was created by Gobelins to appeal to British clients and could be modified to suit rooms of different sizes. The set at Osterley was the fifth (and final) *Tenture de Boucher* tapestry room to be installed in England in little over a decade.

The Croome Court tapestry room included roundels depicting stories from Ovid's *Metamorphoses,* which symbolised the four elements as personified by the Loves of the Gods. The set here varies slightly, with the result that 'water' is no longer represented (perhaps embodied by the pier-glass instead). The scenes depict, from left to right, *Venus visiting Vulcan in*

The State Apartment

The Tapestry Room marks the start of the State Apartment at Osterley. Conceived almost simultaneously by Robert Adam from 1772, at a time when state apartments were an outdated notion, it comprises three very different rooms.

The Gobelins Tapestry Room (or antechamber), velvet State Bedroom and painted Etruscan Dressing Room were designed as a sequence of diverse styles (French, English and Italian) and distinctive colours (red, green and blue). They mark the only surviving example of the high watermark of Adam's interior decoration complete with the furniture he designed for them.

his forge (Fire); *Aurora, the dawn goddess discovering the hunter and Cephalus* (Air); *Pomona, goddess of gardens, wooed by Vertumnus, god of Spring, whilst in the guise of an old woman* (Earth) and *Cupid and Psyche* (which may also represent fire, as Psyche accidently spills wax on her sleeping lover). The theme of love is further enriched by the many pairs of love birds, cupids, arrows and quivers scattered across the walls.

Furniture

The gilded sofa and eight armchairs are upholstered in Gobelins tapestry. The panels depict Boucher's *Les Enfants Jardinières* (the flower compositions after Maurice Jacques and Louis Tessier). The designs, of children in pastoral scenes, were made exclusively for Madame de Pompadour in 1751–3, their use for other clients prohibited until her death in 1770. The carved and gilded frames are probably by Linnell.

Carpet and ceiling

The carpet, devised by Adam to answer the ceiling, includes design elements also supplied by Neilson and was made by Thomas Moore.

The ceiling, designed by Adam in 1772, bears, at its centre, a medallion depicting *The dedication of a child to Minerva*. It is surrounded by four smaller roundels representing the Liberal Arts – geometry, arithmetic, astronomy and music. All are oil paintings on paper laid down on canvas and were fixed in their stucco frames after the ceiling was painted in July 1775.

Cameos

The frieze of cameo heads and vases inlaid in coloured scagliola in the chimneypiece echoes those above the doors.

Left Against the pink background, woven to resemble silk damask, are exotic birds and other animals copied from sketches by Pieter Boel of Louis XIV's menagerie at Versailles of the 1670s

Above The Tapestry Room. 'The most superb and beautiful that can be imagined' (Horace Walpole, 1778)

The State Bedchamber

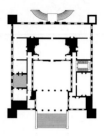

It is said that, upon receiving the bill for the State Bed, Robert Child was so shaken that, once settled, he tore it up, saying, 'No one must ever know what it cost'!

'A very Elegant State Bedstead with Eight painted & Japanned Columns with carved & gilt Capitals and bases on Inlaid Pedestals A rich Carved and gilt Cornice and dome A rich Japanned & highly carved and gilt headboard with figures and other ornaments the furniture Velvet Drapery richly embroidered in Colours the Dome inside lined with green Silk embroidered with festoon and other ornaments the whole fringed in festton with rich Gold colour and Silk fringe and Tassells …'

1782 inventory

A shrine to love

The bed and the entire room are a celebration of the posterity of the Child family, a shrine to love, and an ode to sleep. The domed, theatrical, eight-poster bed, so architectural in its execution, is a temple to Venus, goddess of love and fertility. Her likeness, in a central medallion, is garlanded by carved nymphs on the headboard. Venus is also depicted in the scene central to the pier-glass crest. Above, on the ceiling to the room, the central medallion depicts her attendant, Aglaia, one of the three graces, being enslaved by love in the form of Cupid.

The bed corners bear winged female sphinxes, as do the frame of the pier-glass, the painted chimney board and the backs of the six cabriole armchairs. The sphinx is the guardian of the garden of Arcadia, the place of perfect rural pleasure; a theme echoed in the other painted scenes of the ceiling, which depict the pleasures of pastoral life. The green palette of the room (described as apple green by a visitor in 1788),

Below left Green velvet bed-hangings showing the alternating emblems of poppy heads and the Childs' eagle

Below right The State Bedchamber ceiling depicting Aglaia enslaved by love

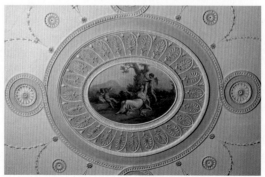

a colour preferred for bedrooms, is also associated with spring and fertility.

The green bed valance alternates embroidered eagles with adders in their beaks (crest of the Child family) and poppy heads (emblem of sleep). An abundance of embroidered floral imagery can be seen above and below it, and rosettes and bell flowers decorate the bed carpet, wall and door friezes,

overmantel mirror and curtain pelmets.

Walpole, during his second visit to the house in 1778, commented unfavourably on the artificial flowers festooned around the bed dome 'like a modern head-dress'. The silk flowers that decorate the dome today were remade in the 1980s, while the wall coverings date from the 1950s – a poor substitute for the rich green velvet listed in Adam's time.

Above left Adam's design for the State Bed of 1776 (Sir John Soane's Museum)

Above right The State Bed

The Etruscan Dressing Room

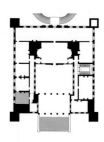

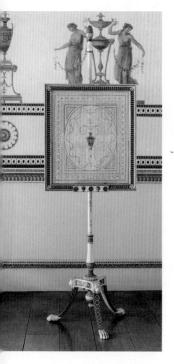

Few rooms are more completely decorated than this.

Adam's 'total design' approach is evident in the painted wall decoration and door panels; the ceiling design and armchairs; the chimney board and fire-screen; and even the embroidered needlework panel that it holds (executed by Mrs Child herself). Alas, the carpet he also designed was probably never executed.

Vasemania

The inspiration for the decoration probably came from several contemporary sources. The first was the collection of Sir William Hamilton (1730–1803). Hamilton had served as envoy-extraordinary to the Spanish court at Naples and while there amassed a collection of art and antiquities including pictures, bronzes, terracottas and archaeological finds from the local excavations of the time, especially ancient vases. Those who visited him in Italy came back with tales of the magnificence of his collection, and he himself commissioned colour-illustrated books about his purchases. The fashion spread. An engraving from Hamilton's *Vases, Scene in the Garden of Hesperides,* is even painted on the black and gold japanned pembroke table in this room.

By 1769 Josiah Wedgwood (1730–95) had opened his pottery works, Etruria, in Staffordshire and began producing vases based on Hamilton's publications. In time his range of vases grew to include those imitating black basalt (a dark volcanic rock), ornamented in bas-relief or painted in imitation of Greek and Roman red-figure vases. These he displayed in his London showrooms, creating a 'violent Vase Madness' among the fashionable. Not surprisingly, Walpole described Adam's room as 'painted all over like Wedgwood's ware' in 1778.

Piranesi

The Italian artist Giovanni Battista Piranesi's (1720–78) 1769 publication *Diverse maniere d'adornare i cammini (Different ways of decorating rooms)* may also have provided source material. Adam had met Piranesi during his Grand Tour and greatly admired him. Illustrations from this work not only explained his 'archaeological gaze',

Above The Etruscan Dressing Room fire-screen, the design by Adam and the panel embroidered on by Mrs Child

Right Detail of one of the painted armchairs

but also aimed 'to show what use an able architect may make of the ancient monuments by properly adapting them to our own manners and customs'.

Etruscan rooms

Adam claimed that he had had the idea of applying the style of ornament and colouring found on ancient Greek and Etruscan vases to decorate contemporary interiors. He created five Etruscan rooms in total.

At Osterley the decoration (on the walls, ceiling and matching chimney board) was produced by Pietro Maria Borgnis (?1742–c.1810),

an Italian ornament painter who had almost certainly travelled to England with his father at the invitation of Sir Francis Dashwood, for whom they worked at West Wycombe Park. He painted the ornaments on sheets of paper, which were then pasted onto canvas and fixed to the walls and ceiling. Adam produced a drawing for the chairs in 1776, revising the design, which had included terracotta ornaments on a black background, shortly after; the design drawing for the pier-glass the year before. Its black and gold border reflects the decoration of the oriental lacquer on the commode beneath.

Above The Etruscan Dressing Room

1. The South Corridor

Three generations of the Child family were intimately involved with the East India Company.

Sir Francis the Elder had been a substantial stockholder in the old East India Company, while his son, Robert, was elected Director and Deputy Chairman in the same year he was knighted – 1714. His brother, Francis the Younger, also served as a Director, while their youngest brother, Samuel, left £45,000 of EIC company stock to his wife, and £3,000 to his eldest son, Francis, when he died in 1752. In the second half of the 18th century there were also three company ships named after Osterley.

Lacquer furniture

Like many contemporary European collectors, the Child family was influenced by the tastes and styles of the countries with which the East India Company traded. Lacquerware, with its polished lustre and exotic luxury, was particularly popular. Agneta Yorke, visiting Osterley in the 1770s, commented on the 'profusion of rich China & Japan' – so much that she 'could almost fancy [herself] in Pekin'.

Right The lacquer hall chairs, bearing the Child arms, were probably made in China in the 1720s for Sir Francis Child the Younger

This passage displays some of the large suite of Chinese black and gold lacquer furniture which bears the arms of the Childs of Worcester and London, and which was almost certainly commissioned in China and made for Sir Francis Child the Younger in the 1720s.

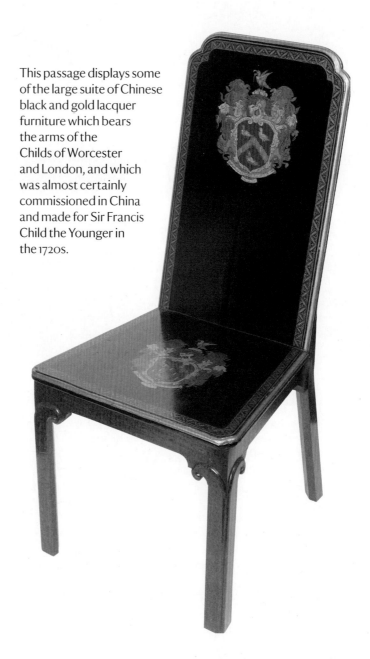

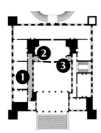

2 and 3. The South and North Vestibules

Paintings

Also to be found along this corridor is the painting *Temple Bar (The May Day Procession)* (early 1770s) by John Collett (c.1725–80); see p.6. Child & Co. Bank was based at 1 Fleet Street, immediately adjacent to Temple Bar (the business even made use of some of the monument's interior for storage). Consequently, images of the Bar were often used by Child & Co., including on the bank notes that it issued. This painting was probably commissioned for display in the family's bank. It depicts the annual May Day procession, with chimney sweeps dancing in the street, milk maids dressed for spring in pinks and blues, fashionable gentlemen and a wooden-legged fiddler.

Other paintings include *Osterley from the South-East* and *Osterley from the South-West* (1784) by Anthony Devis (1729–1816) and two portraits of the sons of Sir Francis Child the Elder and his wife Elizabeth Wheeler by Mary Beale (1633–97).

Two vestibules join the north and south passages of the principal floor with the Entrance Hall.

Porcelain

Today, the Vestibules are used to display part of the Childs' large collection of porcelain. Some of these items were certainly in their London home, 38 Berkeley Square, in 1860, when an inventory was taken. These include a Sèvres ewer and cover with *bleu-céleste* (sky blue) backgrounds decorated with trophies and classical quotations of love. These were possibly made as a gift to the future Kings of France Louis XVIII or Charles X on their weddings in 1771 and 1773 respectively.

Below A pear-shaped Sèvres porcelain ewer and attached cover with *bleu-céleste* background, 1770

The North Corridor and Great Stair

This is the principal staircase, which rises from the ground floor's family entrance to the bedroom floor.

It was decorated in two stages, with Corinthian columns on the *piano nobile*, and Ionic ones on the floor above, as well as the friezes and panels of large-scale stucco ornaments, including ewers and vases emblematic of hospitality. The balusters are identical to those designed by Adam for Kenwood and were described in the 1770s as being painted 'fair blue'.

Above The handrail and baluster of the Great Stair

Right The Great Stair with its Corinthian columns

Opposite The ceiling of the Great Stair is filled with a painted copy of *The Apotheosis of the Duke of Buckingham* after Rubens

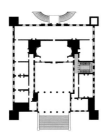

Triumph of a royal favourite

On the ceiling above is a painted copy of *The Apotheosis of the Duke of Buckingham* after Peter Paul Rubens (1577–1640). Sir Francis Child the Elder was involved in the Treaty of Ryswick of 1697, which ended the Nine Years War with France and Spain. The same year he travelled through the Netherlands, Flanders and Germany, buying a great many decorative objects and over 60 paintings, including Rubens's *The Apotheosis of the Duke of Buckingham,* which had been commissioned by the Duke in 1625 for his London residence, York House.

Sir Francis hung the work on the stairs of his London home, 42 Lincoln's Inn Fields. When the house was sold in 1767, the paintings were moved to Osterley and, the following year, Adam made a new design for the Great Stair ceiling, into which the *Apotheosis* was placed. Sadly, the original was removed in 1949 and later destroyed by fire. Fortunately, Rubens made a preparatory sketch for the work (now in the National Gallery), on which this is based.

The painting depicts George Villiers, Duke of Buckingham (1592–1628), a powerful favourite of Charles I, carried by Minerva and Mercury to a temple where Virtue and Honour wait. He is offered a crown of flowers by the three Graces, while Envy seeks, in vain, to pull him down, and a lion challenges him.

The Bedroom Floor

'The lodging rooms are in the atticks, and a great many there are, all the rooms have dressing rooms to them, and are furnished with the finest Chintzes, painted Taffatys, India paper & decker [see p.42] work.'

Agneta Yorke in a letter to Lady Beauchamp Proctor, 1772

By Robert Child's death in 1782, there were 11 bedrooms listed at Osterley plus a further bedroom and study for his daughter Sarah Anne and a private apartment for him and his wife, Sarah. Of these, only one, the Yellow Taffeta Bedchamber, contains any work by Adam.

1. The Yellow Taffeta Bedchamber

This room was remodelled in 1759, before Adam was employed at Osterley.

At that time, it (and the accompanying dressing room, which no longer exists) was second only to the State Bedroom in importance and formed the principal guest accommodation. The chimneypiece dates from this phase of works and was probably made by William Linnell or his son John from a design by William Chambers.

Left **The Yellow Taffeta Bed**

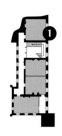

Bed and furniture

It was not until 1779 that Robert Adam designed the present bed. The curved cornice of satinwood is inlaid with green stained wood; above, carved and gilt putti hold a wreathed vase. The satinwood bed posts, unseen under the hangings, bear painted decoration. The bed-hangings and window curtains are of pale yellow taffeta painted with an oriental floral design and embellished with green silk festoons, fringes and tassels. These were remade in the 1920s.

The matching furniture was designed by William Linnell. 'Nine Elbow Satinwood Chairs inlaid and Japanned Cane seats Cushions covered with Taffaty fringed to match' were certainly here by 1782, as were two satinwood tables and 'An India Painting on Plate Glass', presumably the one still found above the chimneypiece today. The toilet table was also listed, 'with quilted Stuff coat with gold worked muslin cover of Silk Veil covered', also with gold work. This was designed for display rather than use, the adjoining dressing room serving all practical needs.

Silver

There are two silver toilet services associated with the families of Osterley, though it is unlikely they were displayed here in their entirety. By 1786 this bedroom was used by Robert's daughter, Sarah Anne, and her husband John Fane, 10th Earl of Westmorland. Fane commissioned a magnificent silver-gilt service from Daniel Smith and Robert Sharp of London for his bride soon after they were married. Bearing the arms of both families, it has been described as among the last of the great toilet services. Alas, it is now dispersed, but two items remain here displayed in the Strong Room: a silver gilt basin and a matching Neo-classical ewer decorated with a putto riding a seahorse.

A second 'Jersey' toilet service became associated with the family with the marriage of Sarah Sophia to Viscount Villiers in 1804. At the core of this travelling set of 17 pieces were some made by the workshops of Jonathan Swift and Samuel Margas. Sarah Sophia's taste was somewhat ostentatious and she undertook to 'restore' the great Jersey toilet service, completely gilding the set, bolstering it with the addition of a Rococo Revival dressing glass, and engraving virtually every piece with the cipher 'SSCJ' with coronet.

Collector countess

The last lady of Osterley to leave some mark on this room was Margaret Elizabeth, wife of the 7th Earl of Jersey. The couple lived some years abroad, Lord Jersey serving as Governor of New South Wales in the early 1890s.

The Countess formed a considerable collection of Asian and Oriental embroideries during these travels, which decorated the interiors of Osterley upon her return. One of these now comprises the cushion covers found here.

Below A silver gilt basin with ewer engraved with the armorial shield of the 10th Earl of Westmorland impaled by the arms of Sarah Anne Child

2. Mr Child's Dressing Room

This room and the adjoining bedchamber were refurbished by Matthew Hillyard in 1759 for Francis Child. Just as he had elsewhere, Hillyard reused materials where he could, but the friezes, window shutters, doors and their surrounds probably date from this time. The fireplace and built-in corner cupboard were probably added in the late 19th century.

The furnishings listed as here in 1782 included an oval pier-glass with a painted frame, six mahogany chairs with blue stripe covers, a mahogany wardrobe with blue silk decorating the doors, a blue Brussels carpet and a mahogany shaving stand with mirror. Sadly, none of these remains.

Porcelain for the family

In the corner cupboard may be found some of the Chinese armorial porcelain made for Sir Francis Child the Younger c.1720–5. It bears the coat of arms of the Childs of Worcester and London, granted in 1701. It was probably commissioned at the same time as the armorial lacquer hall furniture and, like it, was destined for Child's London house in Lincoln's Inn Fields. In the 1820s the service was sympathetically enlarged with matching pieces, including ice pails and entrée dishes.

3. Mr Child's Bedchamber

This room contains a chimneypiece identical to that in the previous room. Like those in the Long Gallery, they were possibly designed by William Chambers and made by Linnell. The bed, the large 17th-century ebony cabinet on a stand, and Chinese lacquer chest of drawers remain from those listed here in 1782. The bed at that time was described as 'A Mahogany lath bottom four post Bedstead and sweep carved cornices Decca [embroidery on satin of the type produced in Dacca, India] work furniture with green Silk fringed', with matching Decca work window curtains and counterpane. Only the valances and bed cornices survive.

The George I white japanned cabinet on a stand is on loan from the Jersey Family Trust. It was probably made around 1715 and is decorated with oriental landscapes populated with pavilions, figures, birds and insects.

4. Mrs Child's Dressing Room

When the 9th Lord Jersey lived at Osterley, this room served as his bedroom, the bed against the north wall. Since Mrs Sarah Child had two adjoining rooms cluttered with a dressing-table, accompanying mirror, stools, wardrobe and chairs, not to mention cut-glass bottles and a long dressing glass, it can be assumed that this room then acted more as a boudoir. In 1782 it contained 'A Japanned Secretaire with pictures and books [and] A very Elegant Gilt Cabinet with thick carved frame containing various India and other Curiosities' as well as 13 pictures. Two inlaid commodes with ormolu decoration and two mirrors with glass borders were also here and were returned in 2013 as part of the Jersey loan. The former, made in the 1760s, of mahogany with ebony, satin and rosewood marquetry decorated with crossed palm branches tied with ribbons, as well as the mirrors of c.1770, topped with stylised shells, are attributed to John Linnell.

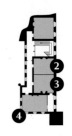

The Basement Floor

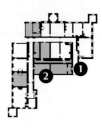

The 1782 inventory lists a host of working spaces and servants' rooms on this floor.

These included the kitchen, pantry, larder, stillroom and 'iceing cellar'; bedchambers for the footmen and butler are listed, as are rooms for the steward, housekeeper, cook, maids, Mr Arnold (William, Mr Child's Valet), Mr Gunter (supervisor of the estate workers) and Mrs Bunce. There was also a billiard room. Those areas associated with the laundry, baking and brewing were to be found in the adjoining Stable Block, as was accommodation for the coachmen, keeper and further staff. The inventory also lists bell lines in a great many of the rooms on the principal and bedroom floors. These were used to summon servants.

At that time Osterley had 22 male servants. By 1788, when a complete list of Osterley servants was produced by the Steward, Edward Bunce, 13 males were listed (including a baker and a 'Menagerie Man' with a boy to help him) as well as 14 female servants.

1. The Family Entrance
Described as a vestibule on the basement storey in the 1782 inventory, this is more commonly referred to as the Family Entrance. When the Childs' London house in Lincoln's Inn Fields was sold in 1767, several pieces from the suite of Chinese black and gold lacquer ended up here.

2. The Strong Room

Fitted out by the 9th Earl in the late 1920s, the Strong Room now houses the significant collection of silver amassed by the Child family since the 17th century – a reminder that the Childs were rich goldsmiths.

The silver includes a vast oval silver wine cooler elaborately chased with floral motifs and wheatsheaf with four supports in the form of lions holding shields; two lion-mask drop-ring handles above. Weighing 1,680 ounces (over 47 kg) and hallmarked 1695, it is the second largest cistern to survive from the 17th century. It is also engraved with the cipher of William III and the marshalling of the Royal Household Arms.

Here too are some of the 5th Earl's racing plate and two presentation cups given to Victor, 7th Earl of Jersey by his godmother, Queen Victoria. There is also a charming inkstand in the form of a miniature Temple Bar (depicted in the painting in the South Corridor). It was

'Presented to George Henry Robert Child, Viscount Villiers [later 8th Earl of Jersey] Upon his marriage with Lady Cynthia Needham by Messrs Child and Co. 8th October 1908'.

Two silver trays presented in 1698 and 1731 are also displayed. They were given to Sir Francis Child and his seventh son, also Sir Francis Child, upon their election as Lord Mayor by the elders of the Spanish and Portuguese Synagogue.

The problems with modernising Osterley

While the last Lord and Lady Jersey to live at Osterley made alterations to modernise the house, particularly with regard to the use of rooms, the house did not give itself easily to modern life. Lord Jersey, during a recorded interview for the Trust in 1989, recalled, 'I always thought one had to have 12 servants before one could have an egg for breakfast. It worked out something like that in the house. I mean you had a butler, and two footmen, the odd man who had all sorts of odd jobs, probably three or four in the kitchen and five servants … a valet to myself … And my wife had a lady's maid.' He sent the cook, Miss Garland, to the Savoy, to hone her skills. 'Being one of the senior servants we called her MRS Garland, and somebody asked her about her husband and she said, 'Oh, I'm not really Mrs, I'm Miss, but Lord Jersey married me!'

1. The Servants' Hall

The 1782 inventory lists two long soft wood tables, seven smaller tables, ten chairs, a stool and a looking glass in a black frame as being here. The fireplace's chimneypot is labelled 'Staff Hall', suggesting that this room was used for meals. It is an exceptionally fine room with more height than others on this floor. It is tempting to speculate on its purpose before the Childs took possession of the house. Might the Chapel listed in the 1668 inventory have been here?

During the 1920s, when once more a tenant for Osterley was being sought, considerable work was undertaken to modernise the services, installing heating and a modern range in the Kitchen. It was overseen by the 8th Earl's widow, who was anxious to protect the historic elements of the house. She, therefore, employed the architect and architectural historian Arthur Bolton, who had become curator of the Sir John Soane's Museum in 1917, to direct the work. It is him we have to thank for saving this room from being given over to heating installations.

In 1782 the passage outside contained 40 leather buckets and a large engine and pipes (presumably smaller than the one listed as being in the Stables, which is still at Osterley today). These were all part of Osterley's defence in case of fire.

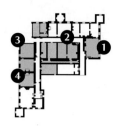

Left The Servants' Hall

2. The Wine and Beer Cellars

This is one of a series of vaulted wine, beer and coal cellars that run beneath the raised courtyard at Osterley – perfect for maintaining a constant temperature. Beer was made in the brew-house in the adjacent Stable Block and possibly piped underground to this room for storing. In 1782, 33 beer stands were listed across the ale, strong beer and small beer cellars.

Here and in the adjoining spaces some of the earliest Tudor brickwork can still be seen.

3. The Steward's Room

The Steward was responsible for the administration and finance of the Child estates and properties: Osterley, their London house, 38 Berkeley Square, and Upton in the later 18th century.

Edward Bunce seems to have held this post from the 1770s until the 1810s. During this time this room was used as a dining-room for the upper servants, and three dining-tables with flaps and 14 chairs were listed here in 1782.

By the early 1900s it had become a family sitting room. Later, George Francis, the 9th Earl, used it as his Estate Office, the south entrance to the house just outside the door affording easy access in and out. A portrait of his uncle, Arthur, still hangs above the fireplace.

4. Mrs Bunce's Room

Mrs Bunce was the wife of Edward, the Steward. Her first name is never recorded, but the comfortable furnishings (including a seascape in a carved frame and Turkey carpet) listed in her room in 1782 suggest her high status; the contents (a mahogany library table and bookcase with glass door, leather-covered chairs and a safe) suggest that she assisted with administering the household, perhaps even as secretary to Mrs Child. She was not, however, the Housekeeper (who is listed as Rachel Holmes), but does appear in the accounts on several occasions. When Robert Child died in the same year, mourning clothes were hastily ordered for all the servants, carefully graded according to status. Mrs Bunce, who signed the payment, had an expensive gown of bombazine (a fabric of silk and wool).

The panelling, which at first looks late 17th-century, has been moved and added to, probably in the 1800s. It is probable that it has been reused.

Above left **The Beer Cellar**

Above right **The Steward's Room**

Below **The safe in Mrs Bunce's Room**

1. The Kitchen

A huge range of kitchen paraphernalia was listed in this room in the 1780s: pots and pans; tins and tongs; coffee pots and colanders; scales, scuttles and sauce boats; moulds and a marble mortar.

Certainly here since the 1760s, this kitchen lies at the opposite corner of the house to the Eating Room. In 1788 it was staffed by a cook (Martha Bishop), two kitchen maids (Sarah Protton and Frances Woodroffe) and two footmen (Thomas Gladwyn and Jonathan Maynard). There were also a dairy maid, stillroom maid and poultry woman. The bread oven in the wall is 18th-century. The pastry oven is of almost a century later; the kitchen range from the 1920s.

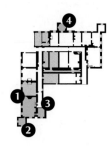

Well fed

Household bills for the 1780s suggest that, while the consumption of bread and milk was modest, meat and fish were lavishly eaten. The fish bill for one week, including oysters, crayfish, salmon, whiting, lobster, prawns and turbot, came to over £6. Some meat, notably venison, was produced on the estate. In 1783 George Otham, the estate's keeper, made several trips to London with the meat. A bill from Wilson, Thornhill & Wilson of 77 St Paul's Churchyard, London, shows the household's requirements for one year's coffee, tea, chocolate and sugar (for both Osterley and the London house) came to £225 2s 4d.

2. The Scullery

The small Scullery was located just off the Kitchen, in the base of the south-east turret. With two large late 18th-century sinks, lined in lead and wooden surfaces for drying, the principal use of this room was for washing-up, primarily dishes and cooking equipment. There would have been no running water to these sinks in the 18th century, instead water would have had to be carried in and heated in the Kitchen. With every item needing to be hand-washed, the role of a scullery maid was not an enviable one.

3. The Pastry Room

Through the last door off the Kitchen lies the Pastry Room. Here a marble slab provides a cool surface on which to make pastry, away from the heat of the Kitchen.

4. The Grotto

Described in 1782 as the 'Stucco Room under the West Steps', this room then contained two long carved stools painted French grey and four matching smaller stools. Decorated in the Etruscan style (like the Dressing Room that terminates the State Rooms a floor above), this vaulted garden room was decorated in 1779.

Above **The Grotto**

Left **The Pastry Room**

Opposite **The Kitchen**

The Garden

The gardens at Osterley should be viewed as integral to the house and *vice versa*.

In the 1780s the Head Gardener, referred to simply as 'the Gardener', was William Deighton. He stayed with the Child family for many years and supervised a team of about 23 garden staff, though the number varied and probably included local people who lived out, as well as some freelance labourers at different times of the year. The Childs also employed James Carel to keep watch over the kitchen garden and orchard (which he did on 34 separate nights over the summer and autumn of 1783).

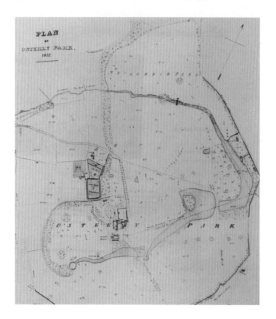

Certainly poachers were about, and there is even record of sheep stealing from the estate. There was also important fruit to protect. Richard Bradley (1688–1732), the English naturalist specialising in botany, dedicated the second part of his *The Fruit Garden Display'd* to Sir Francis Child the Younger in 1732, while Sophie von la Roche saw 'hundreds of pineapples of unusual size' in the Osterley hothouses by 1786. There is even a variety of sweet apple called the Osterley Pippin.

Views out from the windows of the Adam interiors were carefully considered (the internal decoration often echoing the flowers and nature to be seen outside). Equally, the mansion was to be perceived as a backdrop to the landscape, glimpsed through shrubbery from the Long Walk or framed by trees across carefully managed views. A great deal of work has therefore been done to restore this historic relationship between the house and garden, and to present both close to their late 18th-century incarnation (although the best plan we possess is a little later, of 1832).

Garden parties

The late 19th and early 20th centuries saw regular garden parties at Osterley, tennis played on the court (now gone) and boating. Even during the last years of the 7th Earl, who enjoyed being pushed round the garden in his Bath chair, Osterley continued to entertain. His grandson took a keen interest during his ownership, offering the estate as a home for the collection of trees and plants with historical associations proposed by Sir Stephen Tallents.

'The tall elms fling their shadows across the paths, the cattle graze tranquilly in the long grass, the water-fowl splash and dive in the lake … Over all hangs the blue transparent haze known to artists as peculiar to the valley of the Thames, which enriches and softens the luxuriant vegetation of the surrounding country. The red towers of the house with their white angles, and the stone balustrades of the roof, appear above the dark spreading cedars. Up the old walls climb fragrant magnolia and smooth ampelopsis, and along one side of the house runs a marvellous wisteria, which tries with soft green tendrils and purple tassels, to clamber in to the windows and peep at the tapestries within.'

The Dowager Countess of Jersey,
Osterley Park and its Memories, 1920

This image *Osterley from the South-West*, by Anthony Devis

Opposite Plan of the garden and park in 1832

Mrs Child's Flower Garden

Sarah Jodrell married Robert Child in 1763, and the couple made Osterley their principal summer home, living here from June to November each year. She was a lady of considerable taste and a skilled needlewoman. She was also a keen gardener, often depicting flowers from the Osterley garden in her embroidery. The plant lists of the 1780s show her buying the most fashionable and exotic plants. The flower garden that bears her name, its bed designs inspired by known 18th-century gardens and the layout depicted in the 1832 plan, continues to be at its best in the summer months.

The American Border

The 1832 plan also depicts a bed running on the north side of the walled garden behind the stable buildings complex. This was the American Border, created at a time when wealthy and fashionable Europeans were fascinated by plants and trees from the New World. The Childs obtained their plants from the renowned American plantsman John Bartram (1699–1777) of Philadelphia. Thanks to the generosity of Royal Oak, this garden has recently been restored, replanting many of the rare trees and shrubs we know Bartram supplied in the 18th century. They are intended to flower in spring as well as, more importantly, provide autumn colour. In this, they echo the desire of Georgian landowners to extend the seasonal interest of their gardens.

Right above *Clematis × urophyla* 'Winter beauty' in the Winter Garden

Fothergilla gardenii in the American Border

Right below The semicircular Garden House

Opposite above The Temple of Pan (Doric Temple)

Opposite below The interior of the Temple of Pan

The Winter Garden

The Winter Garden was designed by Osterley's Head Gardener in 2010 to provide more colour during the winter months. It is sited in the old Victorian pinetum, which had few remaining specimens. As a modern feature and, given its proximity to the restored American Border, it was decided that any trees that had the potential to grow into large specimens would be American, conifers and 18th-century or earlier. This is now planted with a diverse selection of plants, shrubs and bulbs.

The Temple of Pan (Doric Temple)

Child family tradition believes the Temple of Pan was built by the architect John James of Greenwich (c.1673–1746). He was involved in the rebuilding of East India House, the headquarters of the East India Company in London, during the 1720s, when several members of the Child family were directors. However, it does not appear in Rocque's plan of 1741 and is more likely to be mid-18th-century, as suggested by the interior rococo plasterwork (restored in the 1930s). This decorative scheme includes medallion portraits, possibly symbolising art and science together with others representing the seasons (the animal heads incorporated in their scroll frames relating to the four elements). Pan was the god of fields and wooded glens and companion of the nymphs. In 1782, two tables (one of mahogany) and ten elbow chairs painted green were listed here, together with two large aloes in tubs.

The Garden House

The semicircular Garden House has five overlapping Palladian windows, a garlanded frieze, stucco medallions, Ionic pilasters and a balustraded parapet. It was designed by Adam and built in 1780. In 1782 it contained, among other things, 45 orange and lemon trees in tubs. Today, it continues to display a wonderful selection of fruit and tender plants.

The Great Meadow

The Great Meadow lies to the west of the house – filling every window as one stands in the Long Gallery watching the sun go down. It has never been ploughed, not even during the Second World War, and forms an ideal habitat for unusual wildflowers such as lady's bedstraw and knapweeds, and a haven for rare insects and butterflies. Like Arthur Devis's depiction of a pastoral park in the 1780s, today the scene occasionally contains grazing Charolais cattle, belonging to the Osterley tenant farmer.

The Long Walk

Around the perimeter runs the Long Walk, a path designed to move through light and shade and afford glimpses back to the house through designed viewpoints. In the 18th century it would have had more formality, with flowerbeds lining the path.

At the far, south-western end of the Long Walk can be found the brick boathouse, accessible by a flight of steps down to the water's edge. Its small, round 'island', like a full stop to the lake, is clearly visible on the 1832 plan of the estate. Agneta Yorke records having seen a 'Sampan brought from China … a very large Vessel' and several other pleasure boats, when she visited Osterley in 1772.

The Walled Garden

During the last ten years we have also restored the Tudor Walled Garden, and provided access to it. It contains a picking garden, supplying flowers for 65 arrangements in the mansion every week. The substantial remaining part is given over to an ornamental vegetable garden, where in modern style we grow flowers and organic vegetables, which are harvested for use in the house and café.

The Ice House

Beyond this, also depicted in 1832, is the Ice House. Little is now visible of this structure, which lies beneath a large mound, covered in mature trees. In the age before mechanical refrigeration, these buildings were used to store ice throughout the year.

Above left The Walled Garden

Right The Great Meadow

The Park

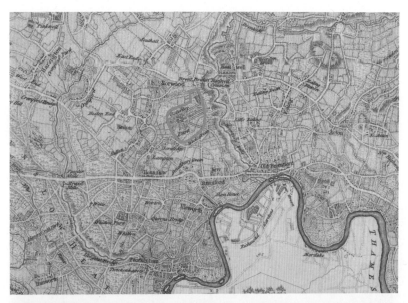

The Osterley estate covers over 360 acres (145 hectares), incorporating lakes, lawns, wildflower meadows, formal gardens and farmland.

It has very little topography, causing Agneta Yorke to comment, 'the park is very fine considering it is flat' after her visit in 1772. Thomas Jefferson thought the ground too level in 1786 (though he did admire the fine herds of deer and sheep). It has evolved with the fashions of the day and the needs of the estate – today providing a much used and enjoyed outdoor space for Osterley's locals and visitors, with ample space for both quiet picnics and invigorating sport. As London has expanded, and the surrounding countryside shrunk, it has also become an increasingly important site for wildlife. Hedgehogs, woodpeckers, five species of bats and three of owls can all be found here, while many birds of prey use the estate as hunting grounds, and bees, butterflies and other insects enjoy the flowers.

A formal landscape
By 1741, when John Rocque drew a map of the estate, Gresham's 'well wooded' park, 'garnished with manie faire ponds', had changed into

Left above John Rocque's plan of 1741

Left below *Osterley from the South-East;* by Anthony Devis

a formal landscape. In imitation of the leading taste and the order of court and aristocratic society, grand tree-lined avenues and long axial vistas radiated from the house. Walking round a garden was much enjoyed by polite society at this time. Straight avenues, linear planning and formal canals, all provided interest and were, ideally, enhanced by viewpoints, glances between trees and shrubs to eye-catchers and outdoor statuary. No specific designer is known to have undertaken this work, probably executed for Sir Francis Child the Younger. It bears great resemblance to the grounds as laid out for William and Mary at Hampton Court, and though the name of the royal gardener Henry Wise has been raised (his partner, George London, certainly supplied trees for Sir Francis's London home), it seems unlikely that he would have created such a close copy at Osterley.

A riverside villa without a river

In time this formality softened. A new type of garden, pioneered by Alexander Pope at Twickenham and made fashionable by 'Capability' Brown, aimed to reflect the most beautiful natural scenes, to recreate an arcadia of grassy glades and open fields. Extensive park planting took place in the 1760s and 70s. In 1774 four cedars of Lebanon were purchased for the south side of the house; 20 Antigua pines and 3,000 additional trees a few years later. The ponds and canals relaxed to form three long, narrow lakes, their curves creating the illusion of a river meandering round the house – a Thames-side villa without the Thames.

The pleasure garden was extended to a semi-circular, shaded wooded walk around the open meadowland at the rear of the mansion; and clumps of trees and shrubbery were formed. By the mid-18th century Osterley Park, as depicted in the painted views by Anthony Devis (1729–1816), formed a rural setting for cattle and deer, dotted with pastoral figures.

It was a working landscape too. During the 1770s and 80s part of the Osterley estate was run as a Home Farm. Beyond the leisured pursuits the park offered, accounts show there was a mixed farm, with a liveried farmer on the payroll, sheep raised (for both wool and meat) and wheat grown; indeed, there is much mention of haymaking in season. There were deer kept in the park, with venison consumed at Osterley and sent to other Child properties. There were also a herd of milk cows and a modern dairy. The estate, however, was not entirely self-sufficient, and milk and bread, apples, meat and fish were regularly ordered in.

1885 saw the creation of the south drive (though the principal entrance remained between the Adam lodges at Wyke Green). This new drive linked the mansion to Scrattage Lane (Jersey Road) in response to the opening of the Metropolitan and District Railway at the Osterley Park and Spring Grove Station. The years immediately after saw the 7th Earl build a series of new lodges around the edge of the estate (Jubilee, 1887; Avenue, 1888; Devon, 1903; Station, 1885; and Mason's Bungalow in 1906). In 1965 the park was cruelly severed by the building of the M4.

The Menagerie

The most famous of all the garden pavilions was the Menagerie.

In 1794 and 1799 William Hayes published a book, in two volumes, entitled *Portraits of Rare and Curious Birds, with their descriptions, from the Menagerie at Osterley Park*. It contained hand-coloured etchings based on paintings of over 90 species. They included an expensive secretary bird, curassows and red-legged partridges, a king vulture, a white tailed eagle, a gyr falcon and a Virginian eared owl. Walpole was delighted with the 'menagerie full of birds that come from a thousand islands, which Mr Banks has not yet discovered', when he visited in 1773.

Robert and Sarah Child enthusiastically amassed and enjoyed their collection. Hayes noted of the Great Crowned Indian Pigeon, 'It was her Ladyship's particular order that this drawing was made at a time when they were in the most perfect plumage.' They hung Hayes's drawings in the library at their Warwickshire home, Upton, and later Sarah decorated one of the rooms at Menagerie House with special coloured proofs. They employed a 'Menagerie Man', Jonathan Chipps, and a 'Boy' to assist.

The Menagerie itself consisted of a small wooded enclosure, a park within a park, on the east bank of the North Lake, reached by a rope-drawn ferry boat. Here was Menagerie House, a single-storey building with two flanking wings with open fronts. The latter probably housed birds behind wire netting, the former more delicate and song birds in cages. The inventory of 1782 certainly lists cages as well as three bedchambers, a parlour and a kitchen. It served as a pavilion in which the Childs might entertain. Beyond it lay Menagerie Park, and both are clearly visible in the lease plan of 1832.

Alas, a series of sales disposed of the birds and animals after Sarah's death, though the park and buildings were maintained and even continued to attract visitors – members of the Academy Club, including Sir John Soane, Johann Zoffany and Benjamin West, visited in 1802. The 9th Earl let the Menagerie, which was converted to a house, and it was sold after the Second World War. Greatly altered and extended, it is, today, owned by the Sultan of Brunei.

Left Hand-coloured etching of a Chinese duck, from William Hayes's *Portraits of Rare and Curious Birds*, 1794–9

'The Menagerie is the prettiest place I ever saw, 'tis an absolute retreat, & fill'd with all sorts of curious and scarce Birds and Fowles, among the rest 2 numidian Cranes that follow like Dogs, and a pair of Chinese teal that have only been seen in England before upon the India paper [Chinese wallpaper]'.

Agneta Yorke in a letter to Lady Beauchamp Proctor, 1772

Above **The Menagerie at Osterley; by William Hayes**

The Stables

The handsome Stables are of exceptional significance.

Much of the Stable Block still has the appearance of a Tudor or Stuart building. Its thin red bricks, mullioned and transomed windows and steeply pitched roofs all suggest that much of the structure Gresham raised here remains; besides which, dendrochronology (tree-ring dating) of the roof timbers dates the earliest part of the building to the 1560s. This makes it the only surviving work of Sir Thomas, one of the most interesting architectural patrons of the mid-16th century, and the grandest enduring example of a non-royal stable block built at that time.

A complex construction
However, a closer look quickly reveals blocked doors and windows, rebuilt walls and a complex constructional history. It has little true symmetry, which suggests an evolution that probably never followed a detailed overarching design. Interestingly, while the 18th-century alterations to the exterior of the house, culminating in Adam's involvement and his Neo-classical double portico, sought to Georgianise the Childs' home, both they and those who owned the estate in the 17th century seem to have worked to preserve the Tudor appearance of the Stable Block. This was perhaps because Gresham's past ownership of the estate still held importance for them and the way they wished to be seen. As with the house, materials were certainly reused and original features incorporated.

A re-used gateway?
The north range, its front façade certainly of Gresham's time, includes a large arched Tuscan central doorway of a later date. Stylistically, it is characteristic of the early 17th century.

It also bears a striking similarity to the one depicted by Adam on the south front of the house in his survey drawing of c.1760, but is bigger, leading to speculation that it has been reused from elsewhere in the house – perhaps from a large courtyard gateway. The western stair tower appears to date from the 1560s; it certainly resembles the towers depicted in Glover's image of the house in 1635. Inside, the stables arcading and cross-walls are later, probably from the 17th century and possibly inserted during Barbon's building works.

Some of the large sums paid to Benjamin Hillyard (carpenter in 1712–13, at the time of Sir Francis Child the Elder's acquisition) may relate to this stable complex. The clock, which was inserted in the tower in 1714, was made by Richard Streeter of Jermyn Street, clockmaker and Warden of the Clockmakers' Company. The bell was made by Thomas Swain from 1753, when the cupola was added. Similarly, Benjamin's son, Matthew Hillyard, probably made alterations for the Childs in the mid-18th century. The entire east range, which originally housed a large barn, possibly open to the roof, was

probably remodelled at this time to include the arcaded screen of the grand stable in the north end, a coach house in the south, and grain bins on the upper floor.

The dairy

The 1782 inventory lists a laundry (with related bedchamber), wash-house and brew-house in the west wing. A new dairy, bakehouse and privies were added on the garden side in 1764 (visible in the 1832 lease plan). Sophie von la Roche visited the dairy in 1786 and was enraptured by its splendid array of white milk-pails and butter tubs with brass mounts 'gleaming like gold', large Chinese butter dishes, tumblers and saucers, 'strewn all around on grey marble tables'. Also listed in the inventory are the bakehouse, coach-house, coachman's and keeper's room; and bills from the 1770s indicate that there were over 20 horses stabled here. These included 11 coach-horses, two garden horses, nine saddle donkeys and a horse for the gamekeeper.

From coach-house to garage

The 19th century saw the insertion of loose boxes in the east end of the north range and in the east range, as well as the rebuilding of the clock tower and cupola in 1883. In the 20th century the coach-house in the east range was converted into a garage for motor cars. In 1994 the latter became a National Trust shop.

Osterley at War

PICTURE POST

CAMOUFLAGE
A Home Guard learns a lesson in cover
at Osterley Park Training School.

HULTON'S NATIONAL WEEKLY

THE HOME GUARD CAN FIGHT
By TOM WINTRINGHAM

SEPTEMBER 21, 1940

3D

Vol. 8. No. 12

During the Second World War Osterley served in various ways: as offices; a training ground for the newly formed Home Guard; an Italian prisoner of war camp (with 19 huts, a dining hall and kitchen erected for their needs); and for food production by Land Girls (for whom accommodation was provided in the Stable Block).

The 9th Earl was working for Glyn, Mills & Co. Bank, a private bank founded in London in 1753. Child & Co. had been sold in 1924 to meet heavy tax duties following the death of his father, the 8th Earl of Jersey (who had died only eight years after the 7th Earl). Glyn, Mills, in turn, was subsumed by the Royal Bank of Scotland in 1939, but continued to work under the same name and management. During the war the firm moved its operations to Osterley together with Holt's of Whitehall, an army agency. Offices were established in the stables (where a canteen was constructed and new lavatories) and the house (where only the State Rooms remained unaffected). The Orangery, meanwhile, housed the RAF Pay Section, and huts were erected along the avenue, beneath the cedars to the south of the house and behind it. In all, something near to 200 staff were based here. One Holt's employee later recollected that the blackout meant a hazardous walk down the drive at night or through the evening mists. The sight of Lord Jersey's cattle – black and white Hereford–Aberdeen crosses (known as the 'pandas') – gazing through the mist, unnerved many a young machine operator or pay clerk.

The birth of the Home Guard

Lord Jersey was also approached by his friend Sir Edward Hulton, asking if Osterley might provide space for the Local Defence Volunteers, a forerunner of the Home Guard, which he was helping to fund. Tom Hopkinson in his book, *Of This Our Time: A Journalist's Story* (1982), remembers Hulton asking if they might dig weapon pits, set off mines, throw hand grenades and set old lorries on fire, to which Jersey replied, 'Of course! Anything you think useful'. Tom Wintringham, a journalist who had served in the First World War and the Spanish Civil War (and worked for *Picture Post,* owned by Hulton),

opened the private Home Guard Training School at Osterley in 1940. Volunteers were trained in anti-tank warfare and demolition, and the theory and practice of modern fighting, from guerrilla tactics to house-to-house combat. They used the Osterley grounds and some of the estate workers' houses scheduled for demolition. The artist Roland Penrose taught military camouflage. Hand-to-hand combat and knife fighting were demonstrated by Bert 'Yank' Levy. 'Mad' Major Wilfred Foulston explained the science of mixing homemade explosives, keeping a store behind Robert Adam's Garden House.

Below Members of Glyn, Mills Bank staff on the steps of the Orangery

Opposite *Picture Post* front cover, showing 'A Home Guard learns a lesson in cover at Osterley Park training school'

Presenting Osterley

'We wish one and all at Osterley, to let our visitors know that we appreciate their care and interest. We hope [you] really enjoyed [your]selves, and we look forward to seeing [you] again soon.'

George Francis, 9th Earl of Jersey, in a letter to *The Times,* June 1939

On 28 November 1949 *The Times* proclaimed: 'OSTERLEY PARK FOR THE NATION.'

It explained that, following Lord Jersey's gift of the house and grounds to the National Trust, a long lease would see the park and buildings managed by the Ministry of Works (later, in 1970, absorbed into the Department of the Environment) and the house by the Victoria & Albert Museum (which owned the collection following its purchase by the Government for the nation). This management arrangement continued until 1991.

Interpreting and celebrating

A number of guidebooks had already been written, the first in 1920 by the Dowager Countess of Jersey, and the 9th Earl had opened the house in 1939 with a small guide for visitors priced at sixpence. Moreover, the V&A had similarly taken over the management of (the largely 17th-century) Ham House from the National Trust in 1948 and been allocated Apsley House (much altered in the 19th century) the year before that – providing the museum with collections spanning three centuries which might be researched, interpreted and celebrated. However, there was the issue of how to present an 18th-century house that had not been lived in for 40 years.

Opportunities to study

The collection afforded great opportunities to study 18th-century life and design, particularly Neo-classicism. The V&A analysed Adam's designs, inventories, contemporary accounts, and the objects themselves. It also undertook paint sampling (using cross-sections to study paint layers – a technique then still very much in its infancy in the study of historic interiors), which put Osterley at the forefront of the presentation of the historic house.

The National Trust at Osterley

Osterley today welcomes over 400,000 visitors to its park and some 40,000 to the house. Despite having been open to the public for 80 years, there is still much to learn and much to do. Our understanding still grows, allowing us to present Osterley in the most interesting and appropriate way both for the property and for the visitors; balancing access and conservation needs and wishes.

Beatrix Potter and Batman

Osterley continues to host events and exhibitions (as it did under the 9th Earl) and is also increasingly in demand as a location for film and television. In recent years, *The Duchess, Miss Potter* and *The Dark Knight Rises* have all had scenes shot here.